ab oet Thirteen Vagabond Poet

Glasgoscopy

by Vicki Husband

Vagabond Voices
Glasgow

First published 14th October 2025
by Vagabond Voices Publishing Ltd.,
Glasgow, Scotland.

ISBN 978-1-913212-41-4

Printed and bound in Poland
Cover design by Mark Mechan
Typeset by Raspberry Creative Type

For further information on Vagabond Voices, see the website,
www.vagabondvoices.co.uk

Dedicated to all my NHS colleagues past and present

Contents

Glasgoscopy

Prefixes

Ab-	Depart from the expected
Agon-	Contest agonist against antagonist
Aliment-	Sustain
Amphi-	Both sides, mibbes aye, mibbes no
Append-	Hang on to them
Artho-	Articulated as they are to each other
Auscult-	Listen, ear to the chest of the hour
Auto-	Refer to the self in the person
Caput- Cardio- Carneo-	Heid, heart, flesh
Clavic-	Holds keys
Crypt- Cyt-	To hidden cells
Decid-	Falling is not a decision
Dys-	We are so easily disrupted
Fossa-	Ditched
Gangli-	In knots
Germin- Glosso-	Growing tongues
Gnos-	Knowing
Hypo-	Deficiencies
Intra- Jugal-	Within the thrapple
Kines-	Move mysteriously
Lacun-	Fill spaces
Laten-	Hidden under
Lith- Luci- Lymph-	Stone, clear, water
Mal- Meat-	Abnormal passages
Medull- Mnem-	In the marrow of memory
Morph- Muta-	Form, change

Neuro-	Hold their nerve
Oligo-	Few communicate
Ortho- Osteo- Oto-	Directly to bone, to ear
Pect- Peni -Penna-	But to breast, tail, wing
Pep-Pheno-	Digesting appearances
Propri-	One's own self with its
Poly- Pseudo- Psycho-	Multiple falsehoods
Retin-	Networks
Rheum- Ruga-	Flux, fold
Salta-	& Leap
Septi-	That which is rotten
Soma-	A body spread out
Sub- Sucr- Sudor-	Beneath sweet sweat
Synerg-	Works together with
Systol- tempo-	Contractions of time
Tono- Tox-	Tensions & poisons
Trop- Troph-	Turns to nourishing
Vagus-	So the wanderer returns
Venter-	From the hollow chamber
Vita-	Where Life is
Vitre-	A glass
Zyg-	Twin

Room

I have an appointment with A. The front door has a fist-shaped hole. I try the handle, it is dark in the hallway, all doors shut save for one ajar that opens into a lounge, sparse, lit by the greenish light of a cloudy aquarium. 'Hullo'? On the sofa a figure reclining under a blanket, back towards me, beside him is a still life: side table from a long-lost nest, pint glass of tangerine-coloured liquid, and a broken lamp. I try my best to make myself heard, before reaching out to touch the blunt wing of his scapula.

Room

B's face is pale, and moon shaped from the steroids. Fluid pools downwards, balloons at her ankles. B lifts her legs as if they belong to someone else. Going downstairs exhausts her, she stops to sweat. We peer out the landing window, nothing is moving, the tarmac is softening. She'll sit out front later, she says, to catch some sun. 'I've heard there's an empty flat opposite, smaller but ground floor, so I've put my name down'. We watch a greyhound lick ice-cream off the pavement. 'I'm stable', she says 'but I don't know how long I'll have to wait'.

Room

'You are exquisite', C says, her face flushed, temperature risen perhaps a degree. We assist her to wash, check her skin, pump a mattress with air, make her bed. I ask if I can look for clean clothes, the top drawer holds nothing more than a box of paracetamol and hospital socks, the others empty except for a single folded sheet. She is not eating, slim as a pillowslip, bones protruding, cannot bear her own weight. C takes one mouthful to please us. We feed the rest to the dog who wolfs it down as if he's not eaten in weeks. 'Don't take my dog away', she says. I ask who walks it and she points across the room at her partner lying in bed, face to the wall. 'The family live Southside, but they've all got the virus'. The dog's tail beats time against my leg. 'Don't take my dog away', C says.

Ways of seeing

The relation between what we see and what we know is never settled. John Berger

By the time we meet, I have already viewed many portraits of you
– portraits in blood, bio-chemical make-up, pointillistic cells – formed
an impression. On paper your heart is a jagged mountain, traced
in pencil-thin angles, you appear as an inhospitable landscape.

Much has been asked of you, and you've answered back. Radio waves
ricocheted through the rooms of you, singing the call & response
of shanties, a magnetic mapping of your waters, sounding anomalies
from the depths. I hear you before I see you.

Here's another in monochrome: x-rays fired through your body absorbed
by the very fabric of your skeleton, where you split at the seam
calcification has embroidered repairs. Remnant beams project
a shadow image: black air of lung, dense white bone.

When seen from 360 degrees your mind is mille-feuille, cognition de-
constructed. Contrast dyes enhance the density of tissue, but nothing is more
in contrast than the speed of thought and this series of black & white stills.
An angular portrait, Cubist in conception, Surrealist in the petticoats of content.

Your constituent parts, no matter how small, have been counted. Abstracted
on a screen you take the form of a list of numbers: red digits, plus &
minus signs. It seems some bits of you are growing, some atrophying,
you pulse before my eyes.

The camera's eye is steadied upon you, within you, pixelates, digitises, portraits are collaged, curated, saved in a cloud. You float, an encrypted expression, one of many selves held in time, in space. Since then, your microbiome has reshuffled, and a billion cells have died and been replaced.

And here you are at last drawn in words, your day-to-day functions described: how you lift your legs into bed, how you hold a cup, how many words beginning with W you can name in a minute. You have been interpreted, translated, filtered through someone else's scope of practice.

I arrive on your doorstep carrying all these portraits with me, wondering if I'll recognise you when you answer the bell. Finally, here you are framed in a doorway, waves and particles of sunlight bouncing off you. Our facial muscles twitch, synergistic, collaborating on a smile.

Room

D admits she is lightheaded when she stands, that she stopped eating a while back, can't remember the date. Getting shopping is harder, since the neighbour got sick. She calls the man in the corner shop to bring up a few messages, but sometimes it just rings out. D tells me she can sit for hours looking out the window at the wind. She is still annoyed at her husband, after all these years, for leaving her. Thinks she should have gone first, with him being the social one. They cut off the gas after that time D left it burning. She didn't forget, she says, just liked that bit of extra heat, the comfort of its blue flame.

Room

'The nurse took my nail off and a new one grew from the middle outwards like a flower', E says. She admires my hair. She shows me how she climbs onto the bed, knees first, sleeps across it like clock hands at ten past seven. I watch her load wet sheets into the machine. The bread is frost bitten, the toaster burns the edges, she takes a notelet of cheese from a plastic envelope. The smell wafts into my mask. E tells me she got up in the night to make a piece and bacon, managed the stairs, next day went out with her sister. Later, E tells me she feels guilty that she lied, she hadn't seen anyone all week.

A woman walks into a city

A woman walks into a lobby, a hallway, a corridor

A woman walks into a stairwell and calls up

A woman walks into a front room, a back room, a scenario

A woman walks into a small silver room and the door slides shut

A woman walks into a room with a blue uniform, blue hands, blue mask

A woman walks into a room of short breaths, shallow breaths

A woman walks into a wall of silence

A woman walks into a hope, and it is pinned to her like a broach

A woman walks into an expectation, a prayer, a doubt

A woman walks into a room, aware that she can

A woman walks into a room and a door is locked behind her

A woman walks into smoke, fifty years deep

A woman walks into a room and unsettles the dust, the flies

A woman walks into a room as traffic, as blood

A woman never walks into the same room twice

A woman walks into a room and its molecules shift

A woman walks into an odour that stays with her for hours

A woman walks into a room, cold calling, with concern

A woman walks into a policy, a crisis, a question

A woman walks into a room, and another, and another

A woman walks into a room with many rooms inside her

A woman walks into a cupboard instead of an exit

A woman walks out of a room, aware that she can

A woman walks into a room, within it is a person, and this is their city

Room

'The neighbour through the wall has been awfy good. I'm here masel. Just waiting for a call fae ma son who's in the jail. I know they get one call and I don't know why he hasnae rung. I cannae go far, the niece gets the messages. I walk up and doon the hall for exercise but dinnae go out, in case I miss the call. This knee needs done too, but whither I'm too auld for the operation I dinnae know. I'm managing no bad hen, I don't think I need ony help, there's worse aff than me. I go doon and back, twice a day'.

Room

Once his heart started to fibrillate, the risk of clots increased. He bruises like a peach. INR hasn't been checked when it should, I make a call. On hold, I watch the cars outside coagulate at a mini roundabout. After rush hour, traffic will flow swiftly through here: follow the perimeter of the park then bifurcate to tunnel or expressway. The other roads lead north and west. G takes the tablets at six, he forgets most things, but not this.

Scope of practice

The good physician treats the disease; the great physician treats the patient who has the disease. William Oster, physician

And it is not the scope that is used, but the person using the scope

And it is not what the scope sees, but what is seen

And it is not the diagnosis, but the metaphor used

And you can choose your metaphors, as you can choose your battles

And it is not the advice given, but the advice given

In other words: it is not the advice given, but the advice received

And the point of listening to the story, is the telling of the story

And the point of telling the story is that someone has listened

And if you provide treatment, you can be the treatment

And even though the outcome may seem the same, you can affect the outcome

And it is not the outcome reached, but the outcome accepted

The scope may look into your eye, but it doesn't look you in the eye

Room

H warns me, through a crack in the door, that I'll need to breathe in, squeeze through. I follow H down the corridor, past decades of newspapers. His fingertips cling like the best of climbers to ridges in wallpaper, door jambs, dado rails, as he traverses horizontally from the sheer face of a tall-boy, to loose-limbed furniture, his pathway narrows through a gulley of boxes, fields of the unidentifiable, the extraneous, until he reaches his basecamp chair. Here everything vital is within arms reach, less important things ripple outwards across the floor: books with unreadabley small print, paid or unpaid bills, things bagged up to give to people who never visit. When H fell, he tells me unsure if it was the second or third time, he was half-buried in old news, the phone was a few valleys away beyond a mountain range of bin bags. But uppermost in his mind was his tea spoiling on the hob. In the background is the faint sound of a smoke alarm's intermittent peep.

Room

We sit J upright, smooth movement has been lost, initiation stalled. We help him out of bed, onto the commode, make him a sandwich and wait. The sandwich takes twenty five minutes to travel from hand to mouth to gullet. Dopamine release is inadequate. Once J is on his feet and started, muscle memory drives him forward. When he stops, he stutters, dyskinetic, reel caught on a sprocket. J's name sounds like a golden-age movie star, his face can't smile but his eyes do. On the telly is something in black & white, I turn my back to it but hear the music's rising tension; peristalsis begins.

How we relate

You, I said, directed to one person, my idea of them. Yes me, he says, meaning his sense of solid self. We, I said, meaning us, in the loosest possible way, humans. We, she said, meaning just some humans, those travelled with or by pain. They, I said, meaning one person. They, she said, meaning not me, not my kind, those others. You, he said meaning his impression of me as he finds me, newly arrived, in his front room. Them, I said, relating to a branch of an imaginary analogous tree. I, he said, meaning living in a state of unknowing, with his various selves. Aye, he said meaning yes. They, she said meaning a number of other people grouped together in a category assigned to them by someone else, of which she was not one. I, he said, meaning someone who just yesterday had been given only weeks, maybe months.

Room

K came back from abroad to nurse her father, then stayed. Now she's moved into this flat with huge rooms, wooden floorboards, to house her collection of rugs, she tells me, as much as herself. And she knows what I'm going to say, that with her new diagnosis rugs are risky. K hesitates at thresholds and edges, has fallen more times than she cares to remember. I admire the rugs, their plums and greens, their intricate maps, a plexus of vines. I move them every which way, these oblongs and squares, to create a safe passage around them, as if they were oceans and seas never to be crossed again.

Room

I follow a river of daffodils down Great Western Road, recognise his house by the garden, let myself in, hear the crepitus of his knees before I see him at the turn of the stair. In the galley kitchen L mimes how to pluck and prepare a chicken, his hands remember breaking a breastbone, wishing on a wishbone, trussing up legs with string as they did during the war. We practice reaching and bending without toppling. The table is already laid for supper. As I leave, I admire his garden. 'Someone else tends it now', he says, offers me some perennial bulbs from a pot by the door. I explain that my back green lies in the tenement's shadow, and nothing much grows.

The Nervous System

I text: On my way, then Bluetooth a call. A siren passes, takes
the on-ramp to the motorway then dopplers into distance as I drive
through St. George's Cross past a conservatoire, Glue Factory,
food factories, converted warehouses, homeless hostels, homecare
headquarters. *You are currently held in a queue* under the viaduct bridge
which floods at the bit where the road dips, cars slow, take it in
turns, carry on, where a left takes you to a canal basin, moorings,
Hamiltonhill's grassy rectangles where flats razed long ago are still
looped by a maze of access roads. On to the lights and ahead:
Keppochhill Road with tall crosses rising up a hill behind the wall
of Sighthill Cemetery, further on – Springburn Road. But I'm turning
left at The Point, angling centre, and soon-to-close Chinese supermarket,
Your call is important to us, Saracen aims north, to the right a high fence
conceals a community of travellers, camped now on concrete, *If you are
experiencing a life threatening emergency*, just beyond here the chapel and
its household, then the new flats where retired nuns live, Possilpark
Health Centre, and take-aways, newsagents, nail bars, public bars,
licensed grocers, opticians, Turkish Barber, Baghdad Bakers, Aqua
Dental, solicitors, funeral care, and chemists with their vans relaying
medications around the city, *hang up and dial* 999 people criss-crossing,
pulsing, shop to pub to the kink in the road, concrete steps the police
call the beer garden, onto the junction with Hawthorn Street, *For minor
ailments* where Saracen Street becomes Balmore Road, the lights change
through their pre-programmed sequence, before I press the clutch and
the engine restarts, past the Speedway mural and KILT HIRE £29,
retirement complexes, across from the new station is the old station that
became a bookmakers, faded sign still visible, then derelict, shrubs exiting
the roof, windows, doors boarded up, it has been falling down for years.

For eye problems contact your optician as I cross Ashgill Road (turn down here for the Milton where streets are named after islands, the corner where I remember a hawk taking down a finch), *For dental problems contact*, a red sandstone chapel, the Lambhill Stables on the canal, barges sliding beneath the street, through the lights that edge Possil Marsh, site of an historic meteorite landing marked with a stone hidden in summer by reeds, pylons bring perspective, electrical lines a minding of transmissions happening across the horizon, as under tarmac. *You are caller number 8 in the queue* Opposite is the crematorium where I said goodbye to an uncle, an aunt and a friend, *Please continue to hold*, past fields where migrating geese rest, refuel, hedgerows conceal farms, tracks, steadings. I signal to turn up Blackhill Road to connect with the top of Summerston *Your call is important to us* a last glance north to the border, flanks of the Campsie hills seeming gold in afternoon light, *Please continue to hold.* A million synaptic exchanges fire, are firing, as I arrive, am arriving, into the present tense.

Room

'There are the girls again', she points, 'swinging in the apple tree'. I tell her I can't see them, but she carries on anyway, says their parents have gone out for the day and she is expected to look after them. M paces, wondering when the parents will be back, stares out at the tree, bangs on the glass. M worries that she doesn't have enough food to feed them all, goes to get her coat. She wants something like cake, or biscuit wafers, soft and pink, tries to write it down but the letters get smaller and smaller until she swears, gives up. When she stands at the back door calling them in, they fall on the grass like blossom.

Room

Roadworks encircle N's home, engines idle at temporary lights and the air is heavy with tar she can smell in her sleep. A top layer is dug and replaced almost every year. N says she used to like peering in, seeing all the tubes, pipes and wires under the street. I imagine the inner workings of a body. I think of layers of skin: derma, epidermis, adipose tissue. N has been sitting too long, buttocks sag from the coat hanger of her pelvis, her sacrum is scarlet, top layer of skin lost to sheer forces as her muscles can't hold their position against gravity and she slips slowly downward, earthbound. I think of the chart in the office, with its darkening colours of pressure, give her a square field of air furrowed by plastic. Then call for the nurse to come with her bag of tender dressings, lint and gauzes, sweet honey tulle, bandages like a long and winding road.

Narrative Medicine

Am I the weather arriving
with a metaphor?

Or a metaphor
arriving with the weather?

Invite me into your story arc,
sit me down, and let me know

how do you take your narratives,
with or without metaphors?

Do the metaphors sit comfortably
or hamper your recovery?

Do similes make themselves
at home, like relatives?

Are you the medicine?
Or the antidote?

Am I the wind, the rain
or the lightning rod?

Given a choice, would you take
medicine or metaphor?

If there were no other medicines
would you take metaphors?

Would you consent to a randomised control trial
with placebo and metaphor?

How are you weathering today?

Room

We look out over the city skyline, the radio tells us there is an easterly blowing in, a high over Scandinavia. The room grows dusky. O's arms won't reach up as far as the switch now so he never puts the big light on. It's been six years since his wife passed, he recalls the maggots used to clean the necrosis, how 'You wouldn't let an animal suffer that way'. In the evenings, O often hears a band strike up, though marching season has long since been and gone. O says his daughter worries unnecessarily, tells me how he used to walk half-way across the city to get to his work, then visit his mother on the way home. 'Cannae believe I'm like this now'. He never saw the maggots with his own eyes but remembers them as clear as day.

Room

The tremor in P's hand shakes ash onto the rug. Once or twice it threatens to catch light, until he stamps it out. He scolds his arm as if it were a child who never learns. The weight is falling off, the tremor eats up calories faster than he can take them on. He tries resting his elbows on the table, like he was told he never should, weighted cutlery, an insulated mug with a lid. Two-handed he lifts liquid to his lips. 'It never stops', P says, nods to the corner window overlooking the expressway. I glance out and see a sofa on the pavement facing an endless stream of cars. 'I gave up my licence' he says, 'when I could no longer hold the wheel. I miss it though, I don't like being a passenger'.

Close

In traditional Tenements sandstone stair treads, worn down by more than a century, appear to soften in the centre as if buckled from weight rather than years of erosion underfoot. Steps, cut from quarried blocks, still hold the impression of the saw's circular blade, marks like ripples on a pond hold energy transferred from foot to stone, reverberate a little with particles in unseen motion. Steps that the subconscious knows the rise of better than the conscious self; a person can trip over the smallest of discrepancies. Walls retain a notable trail of all the fingertips that have sought a point of balance, an accumulation of sebaceous oils. In a wally close, the tiles shine with turquoises, greens, oranges, even browns seem luminous under glaze, drawn with delicate cracks. Others have tiles missing, lost, painted in, some walls all gloss. On the other side, a wooden banister worn smooth by a succession of touch, of grip, may still have the original metal nodules to prevent a hand slipping. For some, the stair is too big an obstacle, a mountain to climb, requiring breath, stamina, muscle strength beyond what they have. Occasionally a stair-climber arrives to mechanically lift a person one step to the next in a caterpillar-like ascent. Have you considered rehousing? I'm obliged to ask, knowing it might mean leaving a home, years of memories, good neighbours, friends and family down the road, trade it all in for the unknown.

The high flats' stairs, that I climb to avoid the lift, have a scent of chlorine/bleach/hash/cigarettes. The walls may be half-painted, numbered, or not, occasionally a fold-down stool at a landing to pause from dizzying motion. Here I put my hand to concrete's cool skin, its Portland mix still gathering strength, they call curing. In this narrow, upright room, where stair rises above stair and so on, I climb up through the steps' negative space aware of the weight above me. I rarely meet anyone. Except maybe a concierge or someone with a ladder, or another claustrophobe. Though in some flats, the lift only goes to the penultimate floor and everyone who can has to climb the last flight. Once, or twice, there is the bang of a door, an absence, and a cloud of fresh smoke lingers with nowhere to go. These stairwells have no windows, only wind-rattled doors to drying areas, bin chutes, and dark stubby corridors that light up as you enter, then dim. At Anniesland Tower the stairwell has windows with views down Great Western Road, smoky red tenements and their back greens appear to ladder all the way to the hills, to Ben Lomond. And to the south, the eye is led down Crow Road, down Balshagray to the river that marks our southern boundary. From the Blairdardie flats you can see planes flying low over the Kilpatricks and Drumchapel, skirting our western boundary, enroute to the airport, or heading out of town.

Room

Air hunger, they call it, more like a drooth, the bronchial tree with dry roots. But what do metaphors matter? Q leans against the wall. I ask yes and no questions, his eyes droop, he nods to say he's still listening. The concentrator sighs in the corner, oxygen slaking through clear tubing, catches in kinks, at doorways. Is it helpful to consider it as a finite resource, to talk of spending and being spent, of running out? Q plans ahead, around what can be done in a day. Eating is a priority, but exhausting. The bathroom feels miles away. I leave a plastic urinal. Outside all the cars are covered in a fine dust, I squint through a pinkish lens of Saharan sand blown thousands of miles north.

Room

While I wait for a connection, a violin plays. Then the curious music of a language I don't understand. Interpreter, patient and therapist talk on a three-way line. We'll meet tomorrow. R's sister will offer coffee in small cups and baklava, I cannot accept, cannot remove the mask. From his bed he'll offer up his few English words. I'll return with a perching stool, a wheeled zimmer frame. He'll describe how it travels, shoots knives as he walks, stops him abruptly with a sharp intake of breath. Before all of this, R says, he could stand and sing for hours.

The Immune System

i	t	b	f	m	z	w	x	t	e	a	r	s	k	z
n	h	l	o	e	j	h	i	s	t	a	m	i	n	e
v	y	o	e	m	f	i	r	o	v	i	g	i	l	w
a	m	o	c	o	a	t	t	a	c	k	w	g	z	f
d	u	d	o	r	u	e	t	h	e	e	k	h	a	i
e	s	n	a	y	x	f	o	r	e	i	g	n	g	g
a	p	a	t	h	o	g	e	n	d	n	l	a	e	h
m	i	c	r	o	b	e	h	e	l	p	e	r	n	t
r	d	e	f	e	n	c	e	f	r	e	m	d	t	o
b	i	n	f	l	a	m	m	a	t	i	o	n	s	c
a	f	r	i	e	n	d	b	c	e	l	l	f	k	y
d	n	e	n	v	e	l	o	p	e	e	b	i	i	t
a	p	t	o	i	n	t	e	r	f	e	r	o	n	o
p	s	a	i	v	a	c	c	i	n	e	j	s	b	k
t	p	T	t	b	a	u	x	a	m	s	g	f	o	i
i	l	c	a	r	o	c	t	u	v	a	t	e	n	n
v	e	e	y	a	o	d	f	t	k	r	r	o	e	e
e	e	l	e	r	d	l	y	o	b	x	l	r	r	n
n	n	l	y	m	p	h	o	c	y	t	e	b	o	m
n	a	t	u	r	a	l	k	i	l	l	e	r	i	w

Adaptive
Agent
Antibody
Arm
Attack
Auto
Aye
B-cell
Blood
Bone
Coat
Cytokine
Defence
Envelope
Fight
Fios
Foe
Foreign
Fremd
Friend
Helper
Histamine
Inflammation
Interferon
Invade
Lymphocyte
Marrow
Memory
Microbe
Natural Killer
Pathogen
Patrol
Skin
Spleen
Storm
T-cell
Tears
Thymus
Vaccine
Vigil
White

Room

The curtains are half shut, the light sparse, I sit opposite S and lean in. 'Can you hear me'? I ask, 'Only one lung works', she says, 'Mind if I do'? Her fingers tremble as she lifts one arm with the other. I shake dust from a stack of appointment letters. 'I've seen me fall asleep on the phone to the ambulance service, more than once', she says, 'and I can hardly hear them when they pick up. The doctor's is worse, so many options I lose count, and you only ever get to speak to that receptionist who trained with the gestapo, never a doctor', she draws deep. 'In my day if you called them, they came to the house. I need one of those machines that climbs stairs. And a new arm, a new pair of legs, and a lung'.

Room

'Cannae say I've got a good leg', T says, at the top of the stair. 'This one', she points to her left, 'hasn't worked since I don't know when, the other is almost as bad. I've no been doon fir half a year, but I'm determined to see ma son again. He's in a home a mile away, propels his own wheelchair noo, but he can't get up and I cannae get doon. Whit a pair. Don't get me wrong, the staff are great, he loves it there, but I'm still his mammie'.

Cup

You need to think first of the cup, recognise it, realise its function, form an intent to pick it up before anything else. Stabilise yourself or be stabilised in position, supported weight enables trunk control, then a neurone flickers, initiates movement of your upper limb led by extension at the wrist, forearm, flexion at the shoulder, an uncurling of fingers ready for a docking of sorts, which requires proprioception, sight will aid alignment of hand to cup, sensation recognises it's there, there in your hand, and you need to know when and how to grip, to weigh things up, grip tight enough to lift and not let fall. The lift from table to mouth requires co-ordination, so too another sort of docking – cup to harbour of lips, muscles to balance each other out, the pull and oppositional pull of agonist/antagonist, the regulation of tone, the strength to hold still. To hover the cup at your mouth for long enough, as a helicopter pilot knows, takes some work. Then the descent, preferably controlled, to avoid the crash that a simple release of power would cause, finding the table, remembering where it was before.

Room

V sits at his window overlooking a junction on the brow of the hill. He hasn't heard me come in, so I put my head around the living room door and ask if I can, introduce myself again. 'You look familiar', he says, has a vague recollection of my face, the uniform, welcomes me anyway. 'It's not what I forget, but what I remember that's the problem'. He tells me how the whales suffered, how he regrets that second season on the ships, but for the money. We burn some toast and make cold tea. V talks tenderly of his son, long since grown, and then again of the whales that he was paid to butcher, that someone else had just harpooned.

Clinic room

BIBA Ax

Hx
Δ ###

Rx
Rx

Ax Rx
Abx
i/v
Ψ

Rx Rx Rx

c/o +++

Hb Na Ca K
SpO_2

Rx O_2
Rx PoC on d/c

Room

W listens at night to it creeping closer. She has a list of emergency contacts, some numbers just ring out. She hasn't been over the door for a year, she is too young for this. Her friend will bring her in food, she says, meaning a packet of crisps, dinner will be a milky drink she'll throw up later. W worries about surfaces, 'it can live for 72 hours, and the carers go house to house'. She rows herself across the bed, arms for oars, scared to stand. W is worried about falling because the ambulances are caught up elsewhere, she listens to them shrieking up and down Great Western Road, like drunks.

Room

'Baby'! An incongruous greeting from X as he teeters up the hall, trusting only solid furniture, worksurfaces, walls. He's sacked the carers again, this time for stealing margarine. But says he's doing okay, can make his porridge the way he likes it, and someone is getting him food. X tells me he has a shrinkage of brain cells, flings himself onto the lowest seat in the room. Every day starts with a rising suspicion, he's attentive to the radio, the police are tapping the wires; X declines the services of a psychobabbelist. And had I heard the NHS are keeping Russian spies alive? He offers to play me at cards, I know I'd lose. I go to the shop to buy him a soft white roll, tell him about the sunshine; he keeps his curtains closed. Later I find myself explaining how the internet uses data and algorithms; it confirms everything he already knows.

Savings

Wirelesses and radios: antique to modern / Clocks: wall, mantel, alarm, cuckoo, digital / Tea towels: draped, framed, pinned: favourite animals, castles, countries / Fridge magnets: tourist attractions, photographic, moulded scenes with tiny thermometers /Whisky: miniatures, full sized, island themed / Telephones: shaped as lips or Elvis or Marilyn Monroe / Perfumes: boxed, unboxed, half empty / Dolls: of the world in traditional dress / Faux-fur animals: cuddly toys, pyjama cases, puppets / Tea spoons with enamel badges / Model kit aeroplanes / Model trains: with or without landscape settings / Scarves hung like waterfalls on the backs of doors / John Wayne box-set video cassettes / Clint Eastwood DVDS / Bags & handbags: curating their own collections / Books: piled, boxed, shelved, sets of Mills & Boon (pink and blue spines), crime thrillers in black, Encyclopaedia Britannica / Family photos: blown-up, [un]framed, soft-focussed-past to sharp present / Matchbox cars & buses / Paintings & prints: hung, stuck, pinned, leant / Shot glasses / Football paraphernalia: signed strips / Film and concert memorabilia / Thimbles on doll-sized shelves / Ornamental menageries: glass, ceramic, porcelain, stone / Crosses / Calendars: of church, of mass, of Mecca, of the local take-away/ Posters of aphorisms or religious phrases / Maps / Stains in recognisable shapes / House-plants / Fruit flies / Cardboard tubes of spent toilet rolls / Mould / Microbiomes / Miscellaneous

Room

I arrive with news of the weather, Y agrees it's cold, practices lassoing a cardigan around her shoulders. She hates things being untidy, but has nae choice, 'the carers put things back all over the place'. Her right arm is trussed up in a sling that loops around the waist, and bothers her neck. 'Ach', she says, 'it might need an operation to pin it in place'. The carers washed her hair today but it needs brushed. You tell her about long handled ones, as you help her reach the back, explain how we used to give them out years ago, but not now, maybe someone could buy her one online. 'I cannae get to the bank hen, and you can no longer speak to a human being on the phone. Its all computers these days and I don't have one'. From her window she can see up the street all the way to Saracen cross, a bin has been overturned spilling its contents. As I leave, she goes back to doing a word-search with her left hand, tuts at the letters hingin' oot their boxes.

Room

Z's knees point left, windswept, his quads quiver when he tries to stand with us holding the frame. He overlooks the canal, and beyond to the Clyde with its ironmongery of cranes. His partner tells us they think there are lesions in the brain, he nods along, aberrations, messages aren't getting through. Z's thoughts buffer. 'The locks are shut', he says, 'no barges, just cyclists going for miles, bending the rules'. Blooming algae makes everything green. Later when I call his partner, she tells me he was admitted with the virus the next day, that she never got to see him again.

Fist pump

We can't help but live
As the heart's insistent lub-dub will tell you

We can't help but move
As the fist's grip and release will tell you

We can't help but think
As a poem's da-dum da-dum will tell you

We can't help but sing
As any doh-rey-mi-fa-so-la-ti-doh will tell you

We can't help but die
As the finale's last ta-daa flat-lines

Room

'The doocot is empty now, my friend took six but then he died, and I brought the last pair in to roost in the press. The carers complained about the droppings, and I had to get rid of them, the carers not the doos. They offered me an X-Ray, same as ma pal had, see if the shadow had spread, but I said no. What's the point I know myself, I'm running short on breath. I make do with cold food, never one for a big meal anyway. I used to race, years ago. I miss the buzz, watching the clock to see how long they'd take, if they'd make it home. I find the cooing a comfort, it's about the only thing that gets me to sleep'.

Room

B has always washed his feet every day, until now. He can't reach down; we talk about the ways. I peel off his socks, skin blizzards out. His nails have grown so long they curve over the tops of his toes. 'Does it hurt when you walk?' He slips into old slippers, backs long since flattened, doesn't lift his feet instead slides along the wooden floors on worn plastic soles, skates room to room. It is cold, but the heating isn't on, instead B sits close to a two-bar in his dressing gown. B curses, for the legs that won't work and the brain that won't work. He used to work on the radio, can't believe that its come to this. Then he curses for the curses.

Cold room

This curated space is notable for its temporary exhibits, or lack of,
undated spills, half-filled jars – reminiscent of anatomy museum shelves –
containing unique microbiomes. Although everything ages, even moulded
white plastic, we try not to let it. Preserved in the dark and briefly illuminated
this room is a memory that degrades each time we revisit. One lady told me
she'd sold her fridge because she didn't like her food cold, it set her teeth
on edge and ached in her belly; her kitchen ripened in summer. Most of us try
to keep things a little longer. When I open someone's refrigerator, I wonder
what I might find: a box of ashes, a framed photograph, one glove, a ticking
watch, favourite sweater, handwritten letters, milk teeth, a phial of sand, holy
water, glass magnifying a top & bottom smile, a last dram, a last word, the seal
opening like a musical box to reveal a song that starts half-way through
as though we're interrupting, footlights burning, a ninety-year-old ballerina,
swan again, feathers for fingers, impossible legs twirling as if she had never not.

Room

I am welcomed in, the front door locked behind me, I slip off my shoes in the corridor, pass three shut doors with muffled noises beyond them, meet C smiling in the lounge where she sleeps on the floor to ease her pain. After her son answers the qustions, C and I speak the language of body and gesture, she insists that I sit while calling to her family to attend to me. Three times I politely refuse a drink, some food. C barely eats herself but watches intently as I gulp down a glass of juice, open the wrapping of a small cake.

Room

E shows me the bath that he lay in all night, his partner (who couldn't hear him shouting) sits quietly. The bath sides were a sheer mountain face, he says, he kept slipping back down. 'And tae think I used to climb aw those munros'. When his partner came in she got a right shock, went to ask the neighbour to help, a tall lad, six foot. 'When I wis hauled oot ma hauns were cold and crinkly'. I notice the walls blooming with mould, a rash of grey roses climbs around the window. 'The housing know all aboot it', E tells me, 'they want me to move oot, but there's nowhere to go. Besides I like ma wee flat' he says, 'it's on a good bus route, I can't stand being stuck indoors'.

The Digestive System

Out from under the legs of
the Kingston Bridge, as from under
the belly of a beast petrified
in concrete, its mammoth task
upholding the through roads
of the city, concrete laid in
the sixties, still curing, consider this
as traffic lights hold us back,
releases us as a valve, under
pressure, as we surge forward,
foot to pedal, accelerating
as particle, chemical, cell, we
are input, metabolising. Out of
my peripheral vision a tesserae
of brick, centuries-old patterns,
built as mill, yard, factory, now
dust & slough, re-purposed,
corrugated iron embellished
with spray paint, livid typography,
signatures all but saying *I was,*
for a moment, right here, passing
through, fading. Street lamps
punctuate distance, a bridge
from here to – suddenly
a smooth-muscle-pink oesophagus
with PEOPLE MAKE crosses
overhead and we are swallowed
by forward motion, vanishing

into the future as people exchange
energy make a concert hall to
look like a spaceship, a hospital
to look like a space station, people
make viewing towers and air quality
monitors, 360-degree CCTV to process
& be processed. Overhead electrified
lines, gantries with service ladders,
people follow chevrons, take guidance
from dotted lines, autonomic, reflexive,
too fast to register, roads spit us out,
excrete vehicles, as BLOOD on a
motorbike overtakes in the outside lane
on its way to be transfused, overseen
by 74 sheeter billboards impossible to
ignore, our eyes consuming designer
desires, buyable lifestyles in bite-sized
pixels. To the right: climbers analogue
a stone wall, grip by grip. As light
drops signs glow white, a stack of
student flats are an illuminated hive.
People eat and are eaten from
the inside out, people make their
very own microbiomes, co-existing
worlds, to protect themselves, people
cross paths in tilting trains, slalom on
bikes over bridges where stairs offer
no preference of direction, where stairs

prohibit self-propulsion. Lorries carry
trucks, trucks tow cars, caravans give backies
to bicycles, hearses carry coffins, coffins
carry our bodies, and so on, on a parallel
road a take-away pizza scooter overtakes
a pedestrian as they both pass bricked-up
arches, painted, hollow, inhabited by
machinery. Don't be distracted by a voice
on the radio telling you a gut transplant
can alter behaviour, can alter mood. Open
the window to let out the heat your body
has generated. On the other side of
the river a frigate, under wraps, is slowly
being assembled, cranes nod to cherry-pickers.
At 50 miles per hour I am both static and
in motion, my body's engine contantly
running as, seated, I'm propelling through
space-time. All of us are throughput.
Dumbarton is announced in sans serif.
No alternative. FOLLOW DIVERSION.
North to the dump where gulls circle
our output, our waste. Gulls take
circuitous routes on currents. People
take the off ramp, a slip road to Crow Road
directly north and on to Anniesland,
the Switchback and boundary, REDUCE
SPEED NOW, a facade of cameras, one eye,
many eyes watching its feed, 40 ahead

(no-one adheres) cross lanes to exit to
pockets of grass in between, wildlife living
on the brink, living with noise, with dirt, change
lanes. No turning, off-ramps dead-end.
Take the slip to reach the island roundabout
at Whiteinch, oasis of slim birches, Scots pine
climb through a triangle of light in the gap
where two roads on stilts converge above
a pebble beach, long grass conceals
castaways and graves, overlooked by
tenements, and ghosts of tenements.

Room

'I've no the breath today hen, go up yirsel, I'm sure the wall is solid'. As I climb the stair the sound of chirruping grows louder. The room beside the bathroom has a sign: *keep this door closed*. As I chap the wall, the birds quieten, just the odd tweet, I listen to them listening to me. 'Canaries', H says when I go back down, 'used to keep them at the bottom of the garden but I fell that many times on the path, that the wife put them in the back room. The wife used to feed them, before she died, she went into that new hospital and never came oot alive. All those single rooms, said she never saw a soul. My neighbour over the wall helps, but its no fair on him. Sooner or later I'm going to have to let them go'.

Room

The walls of her bedroom are a faded pink. J invites me in with the wave a hand. She is sat up in bed in a pink nightie, among pink bed clothes. I sit on a round velvet dressing stool. J's hands talk softly, fine finger movements describe detail, while her arms generalise. I have read of what is growing inside her, the spreading edges. J's mouth makes shapes but little sound. In her throat her tongue attempts to seal the passageway for the *ng* in *finding* as in *finding* the right word or *beginning* as in *beginning* again.

15-Minute City

The fifteen minute city is twenty minutes away / is down
a flight of stairs / is potholed / uneven / has no drop kerbs /
no tactile paving / no crossings / no central refuge / an air
of particulates higher than permitted / has decibels to make
your anvils clang / has no signal / is poorly lit / has no
toilets / no accessible toilets / has two Big Issue sellers and
a beggar / three bookies and an offie in a hatch / four shop
units for let / grill shutters on the shutters / has dog prints
in the concrete / few transport links / is twenty five minutes
away / no fresh fruit and veg / has beige food / frozen food
/ has a commemorative stone but no one could tell you what
it's for / has a famous local artefact on display in a museum
an hour away / no post office, no library / doesn't know the
last time it saw a butcher's, a baker's / has bikes slaloming
along pavements / a shared lane more suited to 4x4s than
mobility scooters & powered chairs / a lane that stops short
of / riddled with broken glass / is half an hour away / no one
knows you there / everyone knows you there / wouldn't be
seen dead there / all the stone buildings boarded up
a while back / did have a hairdresser's in a café / a nail bar in
a shoe repairs / a locksmith in a key-cutters that unlocked
phones / has a gauntlet of an underpass / local spots named
for the junkies, the alkies, the birders, the train spotters, the
doggers, the skate-boarders / has a pub that hosts a wake
every week / a few lampposts tied with faded flowers in
cellophane / football scarves braided into railings / has spots
that people have their own names for / that are unnamed but
alluded to / avoided / is thirty five minutes away / under a

flight path / downwind of a sewage works / has CCTV with known blind-spots / tyre marks scorched on the tarmac but no memory of where they came from / metal grills on the chapel, the church, the temple, the mosque / no disabled parking / has a police presence Friday nights at the takeaway / an exterminator visits Tuesdays / an ice cream van most days of the year / distant sound of Yankee-Doodle played as a slow air / is forty minutes away / is overlooked by a cemetery on a steep hill / has bird spikes on the window ledges / armrests on the benches / needs armrests on the benches / has no seating / no electrical charge points / local migrations of school kids and starlings and racing pigeons to set your watch by / has a park with a few rose bushes and no roses / is used as a short cut / has a reputation / is too far away / had resident parakeets once, until the sparrowhawks

Room

I sail into view, K says, a figure in blue at the periphery of her vision, my voice arriving as if by water and mooring here a while in her sitting room. K tries to place my voice, geographically speaking, pin down my port of origin, blended accent, as my vowels get pulled by the gravity of her highland tilt, a mirroring of sorts. She's sharp as a tack, guides herself around her home by touch. Her husband has 20:20 vision she says, but his mind is slipping. He reads out the paper to her as if it were a foreign language. K instructs him to bring her things from another room in their two bed flat. Every day it takes a little longer, sometimes he is gone for an hour. She bumps into him in unexpected places, collecting his thoughts.

Room

'When I took unwell', he says, 'with that Corona, I wis laid up fir weeks. Flat oot on ma bed, which is no really like me. Huffin and puffin up the stair, until I hud tae go on aw fours, like the gran-wain. I'm getting better noo, but it still catches ma breath ivery noo an then. It feels like I'm being squeezed like an accordian. I watched ma daddie struggle fir breath wi emphysema and I wis feart that wis the way I was going. He worked in the yards fir aw those years, until he couldnae'.

Thresholds

The rug runner
depicts a kind of
snakes & ladders
in its vine-like
design

M tells me
she climbs
and slides
and falls

The snakes –
Ss interlocking
like meat hooks
The ladders –
braced teeth

M festinates
across its
landscape
down its
floral streets

We walk
side by side
my hand light
on her back, as early
warning sign, sprung
catch, as she
steps, we step

nettle
to bird

until she
freezes –

with a frustration
I can only imagine

before a rose

Room

'There was one in the bathroom mirror', O says, 'She placed a dog rose where my face should've been'. I imagine a flower in full bloom, petals peach-pink, thick as vellum. And when she looked down she realised they'd turned her hands into flowers too, the little bisoms. 'And what am I meant to do with these'? O asks, turning her hands over and back, over and back, holds them out towards me.

Room

The label on the emollient says keep your body away from fire and flame. P describes her legs as volcanic, as I apply the cream, struggles to lift them into bed, relies on the carers in the evenings but once she gets up for a pee that's her, she can't get back in. It's a long night. I ask to see her bedroom. 'Come ben', she says, 'but gie me a minute hen, sweet jesus, one step at a time'. P's bandages are so thick she walks with a wide based gait. 'I've been thinking', she says, 'with all the news, what would I do in the event of a fire, just sit and wait'? She has considered moving but has a fear of ground floors, 'after that time ma mammie found a man in her room, who'd just climbed in the windae and ran round like a rat trying to get out until she unlocked the door'.

Non-essential poem

While human touch is not considered essential, trees enjoy
a renewed focus of attention, their blooming seeming
marvellous; a touch of lukewarm sunshine miraculous.

*

On the roads only essentials travel. Birds consider
themselves essential, suddenly audible after all these years
of competing with traffic, their voices travel further.

*

Billboards quickly become irrelevant, then blank. Nothing
to see here, all quiet. I travel like post, or telegram
visiting from another century. I'm awaited,

like news. A stranger is still a visitor to someone who
hasn't been visited in months, years. I arrive gesturing,
gesticulating in blue, eyes do the work of a whole face.

*

On the road back trees sway, shrug off leaves that pile up
in gutters with clinical waste: gloves make empty gestures, pairs
still clasp each other, masks lie crumpled, blue, expressionless.

*

I assist a man with his slippers, stand close while he pushes up
from his chair. But when he sways, I put my electric-blue palm
on his back, and we both note the small shock of contact.

Room

Q answers the door in her goonie, she explains she slept in the chair again last night, couldn't manage the stairs. I broach the subject of bringing a bed down, or moving home. I can't leave them, she says. I smell meat frying and, knowing she is diabetic ask if she's eaten yet. We walk through to the kitchen where a pan of sausages spits on the hob. She nods to the window, 'they get fed first'. Outside on the lawn a family of foxes waits, the little one yawns.

Room

When I arrive R is already tired, dozing. She has been to Lapland this morning on a sled, through a hush of snow. Every weekday morning at 9am the channel takes her on a different journey, she has the weekends off. Just last Tuesday R sailed through the canals of Venice, with 'a handsome gondolier', she winks, 'and all those buildings steeped in their own reflection'. 'The dead', she tells me, 'are kept on their own island'. How lonely, she thinks, gliding away. Her plot is already bought, with a view of the traffic of the living, of the hills, of the house she was born in, if you squint.

The Respiratory System

Breathe in: through conducting zones of allotments and back greens, botanic gardens, cricket grounds, and pause, before breathing out through cemeteries, bowling greens, Cross Park and Cowlairs Park, and pause, breathe in: through Drumchapel Park, Drumry Wood, Garscadden Burn, Kelvindale Glen, pause, and breathe out through Maryhill Park and Milton Park, Kelvingrove and Knightswood Park, and pause. Inhale: through Possil Marsh and Ruchill Park, Sighthill Park, and Victoria Park, pause, and exhale through blue space, canal side, riverside and roadside verge. Inhale: through your nostrils, boosting nitric oxide, to the bottom of your lungs until your diaphragm pushes your belly out, pause, then a deep exhale through pursed lips, keep going through two million trees, through ash, hawthorn, alder, birch, through goat willow and sycamore, poplar and oak, pause, before breathing in again, the forty percent of the city that is public green space; listen for the soft fascination of canaries singing in Dawsholm.

*

Breathe in: through motorway, and main road, through school run, and rush hour, through alerts from Air Quality Monitors. Breathe in: ambient air irritants, coarse and fine particulates, and the usual suspects of chemicals. And breathe in: through inhaler, nebuliser, oxygen tubing, nasal cannula, mask. Breathe in: the best air quality since the industrial revolution. Breathe in: ozone, nitrogen, sulphur and carbons – monoxide, dioxide. Breathe: 20 000 litres of air daily. Breathe in: particulates measured by aerodynamic diameter, how deep they travel into your lungs. Breathe in: power station and factory emissions from a hundred miles downwind. Breathe in: micropollutants with no safe threshold level. Breathe in: toxins from across Europe, dust from the Sahara. Breathe in: domestic combustion, vehicle emissions, particulates of soil, sea salt, the fall out of construction work, slough from tyre rubber. And breathe: airborne pathogens, bacteria and virus, in laboured breaths, short breaths, on exertion or at rest. The trick is to just keep breathing.

Room

Staff lead me through bland corridors, tell me that S is 'reluctant to engage'. I keep questions short and simple, and in the silences in between I look at the picures he has painted displayed on the walls of the lounge. All are seemingly family portraits, figures arranged in groups of three or four. Every sky is a flat blue, not a cloud, every face round, pink, blank, no eyes, no noses, no mouths.

Room

'There's worse aff than me', T says, dismissing any help. Steers the conversation away from herself, says she's managed all this time, alone since her husband died a long while ago, and it's only recently (the past twelve month or so) that she has slowed up, or slowed down, every task a' bit mair difficult'. I shift uncomfortably on the chair opposite and from underneath the cushion pull out a greasy triangle, hold it up to the light to reveal three briskly hairs, realise it's a pigs ear. T smiles, 'that must have been Rocky's, he's been gone a year'.

Waiting room

In analogue days, when we grew tired of a slim pile of magazines, we opened the book of our hands to read, and were disappointed not to find pictures, instructions, answers – only lines. After a while we would press the open book to our foreheads, as if mindreading, usually to no avail. Then we'd shut the book palm to palm, turn it to check the front cover for a title, the back cover for any hint of an ending, but no. Only veins and arterioles busy with their traffic of blood. And so, we would repeat this for some time, this reading of the lines in vain, until our names were called.

Room

From the hall the sound of mechanical breaths: air in, the sieving out of nitrogen, oxygen being made. Cells have migrated from breast to bone to lung, X creates a cat's cradle of tubing as she goes from room to room. It is a wayward diagram of inhalations, exhalations, breaths cross over each other at spaghetti junctions. She gets back into bed, tells me she doesn't want all this – gestures to the world. Tells me that her brain is tired and muddles language. We talk about continence, and instead of saying 'I wet myself', she says 'I cried'.

Room

The caravan walls are unsuitable for fixing a rail, but everything is close at hand. The bench seat that has no arms is in reach of the fridge, the bed in reach of the door. 'When I ran away to the fair', Y says, 'they became my family', and recites a litany of names, of the ones that have passed on, a litany of locations they used to stay every year. The rain is percussive on the roof. 'Someone will pop in later and bring me a roll and sausage'. She fills a hot water bottle from a whistling kettle, before I say goodbye she climbs into bed, under two quilts and a blanket, under a small cross on the wall. As I close the door, I imagine I can hear her litanies recited as prayer.

Room

Z's son is packing up her flat, they found a place for her last week, but no one is allowed to visit, he says he has regrets. The daytime is fine, orientated by light, but when dusk falls sun-downing occurs, and she cries to go home. Every night on the phone he explains patiently that she is home, she is already home.

Suffixes

Capable of living, yet -able
With reference to -ac
Pain, or being pained, at -algia
Unseen junctures, strengths -apsi
Are often associated with -ary
Weaknesses, both -asthen
Indivisible from life -atomos
And so saying, death -cide
When ruled by the head -crine
I separate each of my selves -cipit
Cut out the smallest -ectomy - elle
Of sensations -esthesi
Later find they carry -ferent
The shape of me, the glue -forma -glia
For the record this -gram
Is how a condition conditions one -ia
Into a medical prejudice -iatrics
How a condition -ism
Inflames the mind -itis
Creates an outer husk -lemma
I suggest instead to study the -logy
Loosening of -lysis
Soft parts -malacia
Do not let compulsions -mania
Govern you, or your perceptions -nom Similarly -oid
Defects of the eye -opia
May allude to -ory
Diseases -pathy

Of Speech -phasia
Like Love -philo
Fear, and other such -phobia
Partitions -phragm
Guard each cell/self -phylax
Grow each cell/self -plas
Your form, your shape can be -plasm
Reconstructed, but don't mistake -plasty
Paralysis for inertia -plegia
Split loose -schisis
The body knows -some
How to absorb emotion -sorb
Apply compassion not compression -stalsis
Arrest your preconceptions -stasis
By coming to a standstill -stitia
We can establish an opening, a rapport -stomy
Cover, cut & thrust is military speak -tegm -tomy -trud
Instead of leaking words -uria
Give them time to ferment -zyme

References

The Big Bang: Communities Blown up and Out of Town

Does Vegetation Encourage or Suppress Urban Crime?

Is it Who You Are or Where You Live?

Ill Health and the Miracle Medicine of New Roads

A Systematic Review of Systematic Reviews of Systems of Reviewing

Planning for Plausible People in Public Places

Walkable, Wheelable and Safe Communities: A Love Story

Deprivation, Inequality and the Dereliction of Duty

Body Size and Sprawl in Footnotes

High Rise: The Case Study, The Theory, its Supporters & their Lambasters

How Routes and Paths can Improve Access

Does Paying the Mortgage Predict Fruit Eating Behaviours?

Spatial Determinants of Air Pollution on Exposure for Pedestrians

The Anatomy of Alienation Among Older Adults

Forty Days in a Food Desert: Malnutrition and Other Maladies

How Managed Decline was Mis-managed

Urban Investment – Put Your Money Where Your Outrage Is

Cross and Crossed Legged – The Case for Public Toilets

Can Loopholes be Ramped? A Local Enquiry

Fear, Phobia and Self-Loathing in Acts of Lift Vandalism

Is Concrete The New Green? An Interview with Brick and Stone

Acknowledgements

Non-essential poem won first prize in the Health Professionals category of the Hippocrates Poetry Prize 2024, and was published in the anthology. *Ways of Seeing* and *Scope of Practice* were first published in The Prescription, October 2023. The Prescription was a project facilitated by Dr. Gillean McDougall at the Royal College of Surgeons and Physicians Glasgow, bringing writers and artists together to explore the archive, culminating in a publication which is available to read in their Library. *The Respiratory System* was first published in Anthropocene, online poetry journal, May 2024. *Waiting room* was first published in Butcher's Dog print journal, issue 19, December 2023. *Prefixes* and *Sufixes* were published by The Interpreter's House, online poetry journal, issue 82. A version of *Clinic room* was first published in Cutbow Quarterly, online visual poetry journal, issue 3 March 2023. An visual-poetic artwork version was installed in at the Off-Page Vispo exhibition, Many Studios, Glasgow, March 2023.

Big thanks to my friend and fellow poet Mark Russell who generously gave editorial comments on a draft version of this book, as well as Suzanne Motherwell for her eagle-eyed editorial acuity. Thanks also to Jim Carruth and Dr. Gavin Francis for generously giving their time to comment on the book, and of course to Vagabond Voices founder and editor Allan Cameron whose dedication to publishing is admirable. I'd also like to acknowledge the support of Hospitalfield where I was fortunate to spend a two week residency during which time some of these poems were written or developed. And finally a big shout out to St Mungo's Mirroball – a supportive network of poets based in Glasgow which I've been a member of for many years.

Please note all the people described in this book, although informed by my twenty five years of NHS work, are fictional.